window boxes

window boxes

Stephanie Donaldson

APPLE

This edition published in 2008 by
Apple Press
7 Greenland Street
London NW1 0ND
www.apple-press.com

ISBN: 978 1 84543 241 6

This book was designed and produced by Anness Publishing Ltd
Hermes House
88–89 Blackfriars Road
London SE1 8HA
www.annesspublishing.com

CONTENTS

INTRODUCTION

Many enthusiasts began their love of gardening with a window box,
for while a garden is full of unknown elements such as weeds, pests and
unidentified plants, a window box is a miniature garden which is easily
reduced to bare earth for you to experiment with again and again,
without great expenditure of time or money.

Window boxes can enhance a beautiful façade and, just as important,
improve or disguise less attractive surroundings.
A pretty window box will divert attention long before peeling paint
or a cracked window pane are noticed.

The Victorians were enthusiastic gardeners and popularized window boxes,
building their villas with generous window ledges edged with decorative
metalwork and sometimes even including miniature greenhouses, known
as "wardian cases", in which they could display their newly discovered
acquisitions to evoke the envy of their neighbours. Wonderful deep win-
dowsills are not a feature of many modern houses and most of us need to use
brackets or other supports to position our window boxes; but one need not
be too literal-minded about this and a window box is just as decorative placed
on a doorstep, on the ground under a window, on a balcony
or on top of a wall.

Nowadays there are almost as many styles of container available as there are
plants and you will find there is something to suit every taste and pocket,
from a simple rustic wooden box through stylish terracotta to the grandest
stone troughs suitable to grace a stately home.

BASIC TECHNIQUES

Seed Sowing

Some plants are very easy to sow from seed – marigolds rarely disappoint, even if you are a complete beginner.

1 Fill the pot with seed compost. Gently firm and level the surface by pressing down on the compost using a pot of the same size.

2 When sowing large seeds, such as sunflowers or marigolds, use a dibber, cane or pencil to make holes for each seed. Plant the seeds and then firmly tap the side of the pot with the flat of your hand to fill the holes with compost. Water from above, using a fine rose on a watering can, or by standing the pot in a saucer of water until the surface of the compost is moist. Cover the pot with a black plastic bag as most seeds germinate best in a warm dark place. Check daily and bring into the light when the seedlings are showing.

3 When sowing small seeds they should be thinly scattered on the surface of the compost and then covered with just enough sieved compost to conceal them. Firm the surface, using another pot, and then treat in the same way as large seeds.

Potting-on

Sooner or later, plants need repotting. Young seedlings, shown here, do not thrive in over-large pots. Divide the plants, if necessary, and plant them in pots the same size as the one they were previously grown in.

1 Seedlings will probably be ready to move into larger pots when the roots start to emerge through the holes in the base of the pot. To check, gently remove the rootball from the pot and, if there are plenty of roots showing, you will know the plants are ready for a move.

2 If there is more than one seedling in the pot, gently break each seedling away with a good rootball. (Some plants hate to have their roots disturbed. The information on the seed packet will tell you this. These seeds are best sown individually in peat pots.)

3 Lower the rootball of the plant into the pot and gently pour compost around it, lightly pressing the compost around the roots and stem. It does not matter if the stem of the seedling is buried deeper than it was previously as long as the leaves are well clear of the soil. Water, using a can with a fine rose.

Watering

Like other containers, window boxes dry out very quickly and regular watering is essential. Watering should be carried out in the early morning or late evening during summer months. If only one watering is possible, an evening watering is preferable as the plants have the cool night hours in which to absorb the water.

1 Watering a large window box with a hose is easier and more effective than a watering can, provided there are no restrictions on hose use.

2 Small window boxes can be adequately watered with a watering can.

Insecticides

There are two main types of insecticide available to combat common pests. Before planting your window box it is advisable to check the plants for pests and, if any are found, follow the recommended treatment. During the growing season, keep a look-out for pests and treat your plants before any real damage is done.

Contact insecticides

These must be sprayed directly on to the insects to be effective. Most organic insecticides work this way, but they generally kill all insects, even beneficial ones, such as hoverflies and ladybirds. Try to remove these before spraying the infected plant.

Systemic insecticides

These work by being absorbed by the plant's root or leaf system and killing the insects that come into contact with the plant. This will work for difficult pests, such as vine weevils which are hidden in the soil, and scale insects which protect themselves from above with a scaly cover.

BIOLOGICAL CONTROL

Commercial growers now use biological control in their glasshouses; this involves natural predators being introduced to eat the pest population. Although not all of these are suitable for the amateur gardener, they can be used in conservatories for dealing with pests such as whitefly.

Planting in Terracotta

Terracotta window boxes are always popular, but need some preparation before planting.

1 With terracotta window boxes it is essential to provide some form of drainage material in the base. In small window boxes this can be broken pieces of pot, known as crocks.

2 Another useful drainage material is gravel, which is easily available from your local garden centre in various sizes.

3 When planting in large window boxes, recycle polystyrene plant trays as drainage material. Lumps of polystyrene are excellent for this purpose and as they retain warmth they are of additional benefit to the plant.

4 Cover the drainage material with a layer of compost before planting in the window box.

Planting Wicker Baskets

If you wish to use a more unconventional container as a window box you may need to seal it in some way to prevent leakage.

1 Line the basket with a generous layer of moss – this will prevent the compost leaking away.

2 Fill the basket with compost and mix in plant food granules or any organic alternative you wish to use.

Planting in Plastic Window Boxes

If you do not wish to use heavy terracotta containers, there are plenty of good-sized plastic ones available. It is also cheaper to use one of these and then place it inside a more attractive, but possibly old or fragile, container.

1 When buying plastic pots, check that the drainage holes are open. Some manufacturers mark the holes, but leave it to the customer to punch them out or drill them as required. If using a drill, remember to place a good wedge of polystyrene or some other material between the pot and the top of your work table.

2 With plastic window boxes there is no need to use any drainage material at the base of the container; simply cover the bottom of the pot with a layer of compost.

Plant Supports

Climbing plants need support even in window boxes. Support can be provided by using canes, which can be pushed into the window box, or a trellis, which is fastened to a wall, or a free-standing frame.

Plants that are Pot-bound

Some plants that have been growing in small pots for a certain length of time can become "pot-bound". Gently tease out the roots around the bottom and edges to encourage the roots to grow down into the container.

Common Pests

Vine weevils (*above*)
These white grubs are a real problem. The first sign of an infestation is the sudden collapse of the plant, which has died as a result of the weevil eating its roots. Systemic insecticides or natural predators can be used as a preventative, but once a plant has been attacked it is usually too late to save it. Never re-use the soil from an affected plant.

Caterpillars (*above*)
The occasional caterpillar can simply be picked off the plant and disposed of as you see fit, but a major infestation can strip a plant before your eyes. Contact insecticides are usually very effective in these cases.

Snails (*right*)
Snails can be a problem in window boxes as they tuck themselves behind the containers during daylight and venture out to feast at night. Slug pellets should deal with them or, alternatively, you can venture out yourself with a torch and catch them.

Whitefly
As their name indicates, these are tiny white flies which flutter up in clouds when disturbed from their feeding places on the underside of leaves. Whitefly are particularly troublesome in conservatories, where a dry atmosphere encourages them to breed. Keep the air as moist as possible. Contact insecticides will need more than one application to deal with an infestation, but a systemic insecticide will protect the plant for weeks.

Mealy bugs
These look like spots of white mould. They are hard to shift and regular treatment with a systemic insecticide is the best solution.

Greenfly
One of the most common plant pests, these green sap-sucking insects feed on the tender growing tips of plants. Most insecticides are effective against greenfly. Choose one that will not harm ladybirds as greenfly are a favourite food of theirs.

Red spider mite (*above*)
This is another insect that thrives indoors in dry conditions. Constant humidity will reduce the chance of an infestation. The spider mite is barely visible to the human eye, but infestation is indicated by the presence of fine webs and mottling of the plant's leaves. To treat an infestation, pick off the worst affected leaves and spray the plants with an insecticide.

Feeding your Plants

It is not generally known that most potting composts only contain sufficient food for six weeks of plant growth. After that, the plants will slowly starve unless other food is introduced. There are several products available, all of which are easy to use. All the projects in this book use slow-release plant food granules as this is the easiest and most reliable way of ensuring your plants receive sufficient food during the growing season. For these granules to be effective the compost needs to remain damp or the nutrients cannot be released.

A variety of plant foods: from the left; liquid feed, 2 types of pelleted slow-release plant food granules, a general fertilizer and loose slow-release plant food granules.

Slow-release plant food granules
These will keep your window box plants in prime condition and are very easy to use. One application lasts six months, whereas most other plant foods need to be applied fortnightly. Follow the manufacturer's recommended dose carefully; additional fertilizer will simply leach away.

When adding fertilizer granules to the soil, sprinkle them on to the surface of the compost and rake into the top layer. Pelleted granules should be pushed approximately 2 cm (1 in) below the surface.

Liquid feeds
These are available in many formulations. Generally, the organic liquid manures and seaweed feeds are brown in colour and should be mixed to look like very weak tea. The chemical feeds are frequently coloured to prevent them being mistaken for soft drinks. The best way to avoid accidents with garden chemicals is to mix up only as much as you need on each occasion and never store them in soft-drinks bottles. Liquid feeds should be applied fortnightly in the growing season. Do not mix a feed stronger than is recommended – it can burn the roots of the plant and it certainly will not make it grow any faster. These can be used in addition to granules for really lush results.

Composts

Composts come in various formulations suitable for different plant requirements. A standard potting compost is usually peat-based and is suitable for all purposes. Different composts can be mixed together for specific plant needs.

Standard compost
The majority of composts available at garden centres are peat-based with added fertilizers.

Ericaceous compost
This is a peat-based compost with no added lime, essential for rhododendrons, camellias and heathers in containers.

Container compost
This is a peat-based compost with moisture-retaining granules

and added fertilizer, specially formulated for window boxes and containers.

Loam-based compost
This uses sterilized loam as the main ingredient, with fertilizers to supplement the nutrients in the loam. Although much heavier than peat-based compost, it can be lightened by mixing with peat-free compost. Ideal for long-term planting.

Peat-free compost
Manufacturers are beginning to offer composts using materials from renewable resources such as coir fibre. They are used in the same way as peat-based composts.

Mulches

A mulch is a layer of protective material placed over the soil. It helps to retain moisture, conserve warmth, suppress weeds and prevent soil splash on foliage and flowers.

Composted bark
Bark is an extremely effective mulch and, as it rots down, it also conditions the soil. It works best when spread at least 8 cm (3 in) thick and is therefore not ideal for small containers. It is derived from renewable resources.

Clay granules
Clay granules are widely used for hydroculture, but can also be used to mulch house plants. When placing a plant in a cachepot, fill all around the pot with granules. When watered, the granules absorb moisture, which is then released slowly to create a moist microclimate for the plant.

Stones
Smooth stones can be used as decorative mulch for large container-grown plants. You can save stones dug out of the garden or buy stones from garden centres. Cat owners will also find they keep cats from using the soil surrounding large house plants as a litter tray.

Gravel
Gravel makes a decorative mulch for container plants and provides the correct environment for plants such as alpines. It is available in a variety of sizes and colours which can be matched to the scale and colours of the plants used.

Water-retaining Gel

One of the main problems with window boxes is the amount of watering required to keep the plants thriving. Adding water-retaining gels to the compost will certainly help to reduce this task. Sachets of gel are available from garden centres.

Instant Display

For an instant window-box display, why not use a large terracotta tray to house a number of smaller pots with plants in bloom? If you place a layer of fine gravel on the bottom of the tray you can then water this to help retain moisture in the individual pots.

1 Pour the recommended amount of water into a bowl.

2 Scatter the gel over the surface, stirring occasionally until it has absorbed the water.

3 Add to your compost at the recommended rate.

4 Mix the gel in thoroughly before using it for planting..

Types of Window Boxes

Think of the setting when you buy a window box – a rustic wooden planter will look wonderful under the window of a thatched cottage but may look very out of place in front of an elegant town house. Bear proportions in mind, too, and look for a window box that fits comfortably on your sill or bracket without looking crowded or lost in its surroundings.

Wooden window boxes
These are not as popular as they used to be. Styles vary from rustic to very sophisticated. Advantages – ages attractively providing it has been made with treated wood, relatively light-weight.
Disadvantages – some maintenance necessary.

Terracotta window boxes
These are available in a wide range of sizes and styles.
Advantages – looks good and will look even better with age.
Disadvantages – heavy and may be damaged by frost.

Stone window boxes
Not so readily available but worth looking out for.
Advantages – durable and attractive.
Disadvantages – very heavy and expensive.

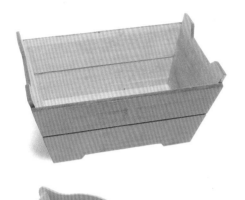

Painted wooden window boxes

These can be customized by painting to make an original and unusual container.
Advantages – your window box will be a one-off, and you can change its look next year; relatively lightweight.
Disadvantages – will need suitable paint and materials and window box will require some ongoing maintenance.

Bark window boxes

These are stylish and wonderfully natural looking.

Plastic window boxes

These are plain but practical.
Advantages – maintenance free and very lightweight.
Disadvantages – not very exciting and will not age attractively.

Lightweight fibre window boxes

These are a practical alternative to plastic, although they will not last as long.

Baskets

These can be used as window boxes provided they are generously lined with moss before planting.

Galvanized tin

Tin has moved from the utilitarian to the fashionable and a tin window box is an interesting variation from the usual materials.

Colour boxes

Flame-red Flowers in Terracotta

The intense red flowers of the geraniums, verbenas and nasturtiums are emphasized by a few yellow nasturtiums and the variegated ivy, but cooled slightly by the soothing blue-green of the nasturtium's umbrella-shaped leaves.

GARDENER'S TIP
Nasturtiums are prone to attack by blackfly. Treat at the first sign of infestation with a suitable insecticide and the plants will remain healthy.

Plant in late spring or early summer

MATERIALS
50 cm (20 in) terracotta window box
Crocks or other suitable drainage material
Compost
Slow-release plant food granules

PLANTS
2 red geraniums (zonal *Pelargoniums*)
2 nasturtiums - 1 red, 1 yellow
Red verbena
2 variegated ivies

nasturtium

geranium

verbena

ivy

1 Place a layer of drainage material in the base of the window box.

2 Fill the container with compost, mixing in 3 teaspoons of slow-release plant food granules.

3 Plant the geraniums either side of the centre of the window box.

4 Plant a nasturtium at either end, in the back corners.

5 Plant the verbena in the centre of the window box.

6 Plant the ivies in front of the nasturtiums in the corners. Water well, leave to drain, and place in a sunny position.

Sweet Scents for a Conservatory

A simple, very informal planting that would thrive in a conservatory. A pretty combination of scented-leaf geranium, deep-blue miniature petunias, purple trailing verbenas and exuberant tumbling ground ivy.

MATERIALS
30 cm (12 in) plastic window box
Compost
Slow-release plant food granules

PLANTS
Scented-leaf geranium (*Pelargonium*) 'Lady Plymouth'
2 variegated ground ivy (*Glechoma hederacea* 'Variegata')
2 deep-purple trailing verbena
2 deep-blue 'Junior' petunias

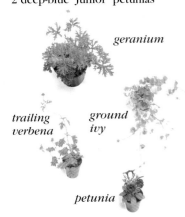

geranium

trailing verbena

ground ivy

petunia

GARDENER'S TIP

If the ground ivy gets too rampant, cut it back. Root some pieces in water and grow into plants to use elsewhere.

Plant in spring

1 Check drainage holes are open; if not, drill or punch them out. Fill the window box with compost, mixing in a teaspoon of slow-release plant food granules. Plant the geranium in the centre.

2 Plant the ground ivies at either end of the box.

3 Plant the two verbenas at the back of the box between the geranium and ground ivies.

4 Plant the petunias between the geranium and ground ivies at the front of the box. Water thoroughly and stand in a sunny position.

Fire and Earth

The earth tones of this small decorative terracotta window box are topped with the fiery reds and oranges of the plants – the fuchsia with its bronze foliage and tubular scarlet flowers, the orange nasturtiums and the red claw-like flowers of the feathery-leaved lotus.

MATERIALS
36 cm (14 in) terracotta window box
Clay granules or similar drainage material
Compost
Slow-release plant food granules

PLANTS
Fuchsia fulgens 'Thalia'
3 orange nasturtiums 'Empress of India', or similar
2 *Lotus berthelotti*

Fuchsia

nasturtium

Lotus

GARDENER'S TIP
This stunning fuchsia is worth keeping for next year. Pot it up in the autumn, cut back by half and overwinter on a windowsill or in a heated greenhouse.

Plant in late spring or early summer

1 Cover the base of the window box with drainage material.

2 Fill the window box with compost, mixing in a teaspoon of slow-release plant food granules. Plant the fuchsia in the centre of the window box.

3 Plant the three nasturtiums, evenly spaced, along the back of the window box.

4 Plant the two lotuses in the front of the window box on either side of the fuchsia. Water thoroughly, leave to drain, and stand in a sunny position.

Dark Drama

The intense purple of the heliotrope usually dominates other plants, but here it is teamed with a selection of equally dramatic plants – *Dahlia* 'Bednall Beauty', with its purple foliage and dark red flowers, black grass and red and purple verbenas – in a stunning display.

MATERIALS
60 cm (24 in) terracotta window box
Broken polystyrene or other suitable drainage material
Compost
Slow-release plant food granules

PLANTS
Heliotrope
2 *Dahlia* 'Bednall Beauty'
Black grass (*Ophiopogon*)
2 purple trailing verbenas
2 red trailing verbenas

heliotrope

Dahlia

black grass

trailing verbenas

1 Fill the bottom of the window box with suitable drainage material.

2 Fill the window box with compost, mixing in 3 teaspoons of slow-release plant food granules. Plant the heliotrope centrally at the back of the window box, gently teasing loose the roots, if necessary.

3 Plant the dahlias in the back corners of the window box.

4 Plant the black grass in front of the heliotrope.

5 Plant the purple verbenas at the back between the heliotrope and the dahlias.

GARDENER'S TIP

Dahlias can be overwintered by
digging up the tubers after the
first frosts, cutting the stems
back to 15 cm (6 in) and drying
them off before storing in
slightly damp peat in a frost-free
shed. Start into growth again in
spring and plant out after all
danger of frost is past.

*Plant in late spring or early
summer*

6 Plant the red verbenas at the front
in either corner. This is a large container
so it is best to position it before
watering. Put it where it will benefit
from full sun, then water thoroughly.

Alaska Nasturtiums with Snapdragons and Daisies

The leaves of the Alaska nasturtium look as if they have been splattered with cream paint. In this window box they are planted with yellow-flowered snapdragons, *Gazania* and *Brachycome* daisies.

MATERIALS
76 cm (30 in) plastic window box
Compost
Slow-release plant food granules

PLANTS
2 yellow *Gazania*
3 Alaska nasturtiums
3 *Brachycome* 'Lemon Mist'
2 yellow snapdragons (*Antirrhinum*)

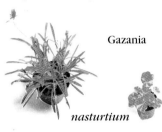

Gazania

nasturtium

Brachycome

snapdragon

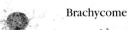

GARDENER'S TIP
Nasturtiums are amongst the easiest plants to grow from seed. Start them off about 4 to 6 weeks before you plant your window box, potting them on to keep them growing vigorously.

Plant in the spring

1 Drill drainage holes in the window box, if necessary. Fill the window box with compost, mixing in 2 teaspoons of slow-release plant food granules. Plant the two *Gazania*, evenly spaced half-way from the centre.

2 Plant the nasturtiums at either end and in the centre of the window box.

3 Plant the three *Brachycome* daisies, evenly spaced along the front of the window box.

4 Plant the two snapdragons either side of the central nasturtium. Water thoroughly, leave to drain, and stand in a sunny position.

A Cottage Garden

Charming, cottage-garden plants tumble from this terracotta window box in a colourful display. The sunny flowers of the *Nemesia*, marigolds and nasturtiums mingle with the cool, soft green *Helichrysum* and blue-green nasturtium leaves.

MATERIALS
36 cm (14 in) terracotta window box
Crocks or other suitable drainage material
Compost
Slow-release plant food granules

PLANTS
3 pot marigolds (*Calendula*)
2 *Helichrysum petiolare* 'Aureum'
3 nasturtiums
2 *Nemesia* 'Orange Prince'

marigolds

Helichrysum

nasturtium

Nemesia

GARDENER'S TIP
The golden-leaved *Helichrysum* retains a better colour if it is not in full sun all day. Too much sun and it looks rather bleached.

Plant in spring

1 Cover the base of the container with crocks or similar suitable drainage material. Fill the window box with compost, mixing in 2 teaspoons of slow-release plant food granules. Plant the marigolds, evenly spaced along the back of the container.

2 Plant the two *Helichrysum* in the front corners of the window box.

3 Plant the nasturtiums between the marigolds at the back of the container.

4 Plant the *Nemesia* between the *Helichrysum* at the front of the window box. Water well and stand in partial sun.

Full of Cheer

Bright red geraniums and verbenas are combined with cheerful yellow *Bidens* and soft green *Helichrysum* in this planter, which brightens the exterior of an old barn.

MATERIALS
76 cm (30 in) plastic window
   box
Compost
Slow-release plant food granules

PLANTS
3 scarlet geraniums
   (*Pelargonium*)
2 *Bidens ferulifolia*
2 red trailing verbenas
3 *Helichrysum petiolare*
   'Aureum'

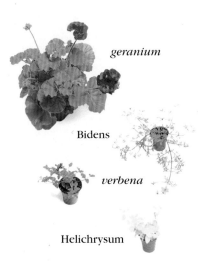

geranium

Bidens

verbena

Helichrysum

GARDENER'S TIP
Regular dead-heading and
an occasional foliar feed will
keep the geraniums flowering
prolifically all summer.

Plant in spring

1 The easiest way to open the drainage holes in a plastic planter is with an electric drill.

2 Fill the window box with compost, mixing in 2 teaspoons of slow-release plant food granules.

3 Plant the geraniums, evenly spaced, in the window box.

4 Plant the two *Bidens* on either side of the central geranium in the front of the planter.

5 Plant the two verbenas on either side of the central geranium at the back of the planter.

6 Plant the *Helichrysum* in the front corners. Water thoroughly and stand in a sunny position.

Marguerites and Pimpernels

We are more familiar with the wild scarlet pimpernel, but in this window box its blue relative, *Anagallis,* has been planted to climb amongst the stems of the yellow marguerites and snapdragons. Blue-flowered variegated *Felicia* and golden *Helichrysum* complete the picture.

GARDENER'S TIP

Dead-head the marguerites, snapdragons and *Felicia* to keep them flowering all summer. When planting the marguerites, pinch out the growing tips to encourage bushy plants.

Plant in spring

MATERIALS
76 cm (30 in) plastic window box
Compost
Slow-release plant food granules

PLANTS
2 yellow marguerites (*Argyranthemum*) 'Jamaica Primrose'
4 blue *Anagallis*
3 variegated *Felicia*
3 *Helichrysum petiolare* 'Aureum'
4 yellow snapdragons (*Antirrhinum*)

marguerite

Anagallis

Felicia

Helichrysum

snapdragon

1 Check the drainage holes are open in the base and, if not, drill or punch them open. Fill the window box with compost, mixing in 3 teaspoons of slow-release plant food granules.

2 Plant the marguerites on either side of the centre in the middle of the window box.

3 Plant two of the *Anagallis* in the back corners of the window box and the other two at the front, on either side of the marguerites.

4 Plant one *Felicia* in the centre of the box and the other two on either side of the *Anagallis*.

5 Plant the *Helichrysum* in the front corners of the window box

6 Plant two of the snapdragons on either side of the central *Felicia* and the other two on either side of the marguerites. Water thoroughly, drain, and stand in a sunny or partially sunny position.

Sunny Daisies with Violas and Bacopa

Osteospermum daisies are sun-worshippers, keeping their petals furled in cloudy weather. In this window box they are combined with yellow violas and tumbling white *Bacopa*.

MATERIALS
45 cm (18 in) fibre window box
Polystyrene or other suitable
  drainage material
Compost
Slow-release plant food granules

PLANTS
Osteospermum 'Buttermilk'
3 yellow violas
2 white *Bacopa*

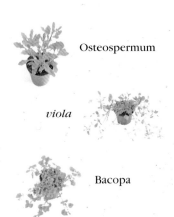

Osteospermum

viola

Bacopa

1 Line the base with polystyrene or other suitable drainage material.

2 Fill the window box with compost, mixing in 3 teaspoons of slow-release plant food granules. Plant the *Osteospermum* in the centre of the window box.

GARDENER'S TIP
Pinch out the growing tips of the *Osteospermum* regularly to encourage a bushy rather than a leggy plant.

Plant in spring

3 Plant two of the violas at either end of the window box and the third in front of the *Osteospermum*.

4 Plant the two *Bacopa* on either side of the *Osteospermum*. Stand in a sunny spot and water thoroughly.

A Floral Screen

An unsightly meter box has been partially covered by ivy and provides a convenient ledge for a window box planted with soft-toned flowers. White tobacco flowers and pink geraniums are intertwined with lavender and underplanted with variegated ground ivy to conceal the meter box.

MATERIALS
45 cm (18 in) terracotta window box
Crocks or other suitable drainage material
Compost
Slow-release plant food granules

PLANTS
Pale pink ivy-leaved geranium (*Pelargonium*)
2 lavender (*Lavandula dentata* var. *candicans*)
2 variegated ground ivy (*Glechoma hederacea* 'Variegata')
3 white tobacco plants (*Nicotiana*)

geranium

lavender

ivy

tobacco plant

Plant in spring

1 Cover the base of the container with a layer of suitable drainage material. Fill the window box with compost, mixing in 2 teaspoons of slow-release plant food granules. Plant the geranium centrally at the back of the window box.

2 Plant the lavenders at the front of the box on either side of the geranium.

3 Plant the ground ivies at either end of the window box.

4 Plant two of the tobacco plants on either side of the geranium at the back of the container and the other plant between the two lavenders at the front. Water thoroughly and position in partial sun.

A Lime-green and Blue Window Box

Lime-green flowering tobacco and *Helichrysum* contrast beautifully with the blue *Scaevola* and *Convolvulus* in this window box of cool colours.

MATERIALS
76 cm (30 in) plastic window
  box
Compost
Slow-release plant food granules

PLANTS
5 lime-green flowering tobacco
  (*Nicotiana*)
2 *Scaevola*
2 *Helichrysum petiolare*
  'Aureum'
3 *Convolvulus sabatius*

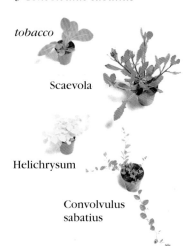

tobacco

Scaevola

Helichrysum

Convolvulus
sabatius

GARDENER'S TIP
At the end of the season you can pot up the *Scaevola* and *Convolvulus* plants to use again next year. Cut right back and overwinter on a windowsill or in a frost-free greenhouse.

Plant in late spring or early summer

1 Check the drainage holes are open in the base and, if not, drill or punch them open. Fill the window box with compost, mixing in 3 teaspoons of slow-release plant food granules. Plant the tobacco plants evenly spaced at the rear of the window box.

2 Plant the two *Scaevola* plants approximately 10 cm (4 in) from each end, in front of the tobacco plants.

3 Plant the two *Helichrysum* plants on either side of the centre of the window box next to the *Scaevola*.

4 Plant two of the *Convolvulus* in the front corners of the box and the third in the centre, at the front. Water thoroughly and position in light shade or partial sun.

Layers of Flowers

This window box is unusual as the colours are in distinct layers, with upright white flowering tobacco above pink impatiens and tumbling white variegated geranium and lobelias. The fibre window box is concealed by a decorative twig container.

MATERIALS
36 cm (14 in) fibre window box
Drainage material
Compost
Slow-release plant food granules

PLANTS
2 white flowering tobacco
   (*Nicotiana*)
Variegated geranium
   (*Pelargonium*) 'l'Elégante'
2 pink busy lizzies (*Impatiens*)
3 white lobelia

tobacco

geranium

busy lizzie

lobelia

GARDENER'S TIP
Somehow, rogue blue lobelias have appeared amongst the white plants. This sort of thing often happens in gardening and, as in this case, the accidental addition often works well.

Plant in spring

1 Put a layer of drainage material in the base of the window box; fill with compost, mixing in 2 teaspoons of slow-release plant food granules. Plant the flowering tobacco on either side of the centre, near the back edge.

2 Plant the geranium at the front of the window box, in the centre.

3 Plant the busy lizzies at either end of the window box.

4 Plant one of the lobelias between the flowering tobacco and the other two on either side of the geranium.

An Instant Garden

There is not always time to wait for a window box to grow and this is one solution. Fill a container with potted plants and, as the season progresses, you can ring the changes by removing those that are past their best and introducing new plants.

GARDENER'S TIP

When using a container without drainage holes, take care not to overwater or the roots will become waterlogged. Check after heavy rain, too, and empty away any excess water.

Plant in late spring or early summer

MATERIALS
64 cm (25 in) galvanized tin window box
Clay granules
5 1-litre (4 in) plastic pots
Compost

PLANTS
Lavandula pinnata
2 blue petunias
Convolvulus sabatius
Blue *Bacopa*
Helichrysum petiolare
Viola 'Jupiter', or similar

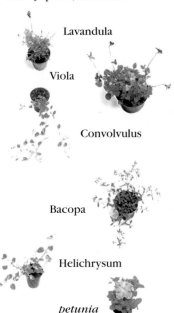

Lavandula

Viola

Convolvulus

Bacopa

Helichrysum

petunia

1 Fill the base of the container with clay granules or similar drainage material.

2 Pot up the lavender into one of the pots.

3 Pot up one of the petunias with the *Convolvulus*.

4 Pot up the other petunia with the *Bacopa*.

5 Pot up the *Helichrysum*.

6 Pot up the viola, and arrange the pots in the window box.

Three Tiers of Colour

Scented petunias, delicate white marguerites and star-flowered *Isotoma* make a stunning layered arrangement. Use veined petunias, as these have the strongest scent.

MATERIALS
36 cm (14 in) terracotta window box
Crocks or other suitable drainage material
Compost
Slow-release plant food granules

PLANTS
2 white marguerites (*Argyranthemum*)
3 veined petunias
3 *Isotoma*

marguerites

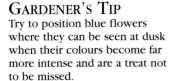
petunias

Isotoma

1 Cover the base of the window box with crocks. Fill with compost, mixing in 2 teaspoons of slow-release plant food granules.

2 Plant the marguerites on either side of the centre towards the back of the window box.

3 Plant the petunias between and on either side of the marguerites.

4 Plant the *Isotoma* along the front edge of the window box. Water well and stand in a sunny position.

GARDENER'S TIP
Try to position blue flowers where they can be seen at dusk when their colours become far more intense and are a treat not to be missed.

Plant in late spring or early summer

A Pretty Stencilled Planter

This small stencilled wooden window box is full of blue flowers. In a particularly pretty mix, petunias are intertwined with *Brachycome* daisies and trailing *Convolvulus*. A pair of brackets hold it in place under the window.

MATERIALS
40 cm (16 in) wooden window box (stencilling optional)
Clay granules or other suitable drainage material
Compost
Slow-release plant food granules

PLANTS
3 blue petunias
2 blue *Brachycome* daisies
Convolvulus sabatius

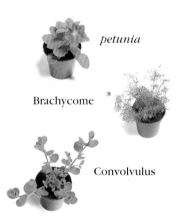

petunia

Brachycome

Convolvulus

GARDENER'S TIP
If you are stencilling a wooden container for outside use, do not forget to seal the wood after decorating it. In this instance, a matt wood varnish in a light oak tint has been used.

Plant in late spring or early summer

1 Line the base of the window box with clay granules or other suitable drainage materials.

2 Fill the window box with compost, mixing in a teaspoon of slow-release plant food granules. Plant the three petunias, evenly spaced, towards the back of the window box.

3 Plant the *Brachycome* daisies between the petunias.

4 Plant the *Convolvulus* centrally at the front of the box. Water thoroughly and position in full or partial sun.

Flowers for Late Summer

Although this window box is already looking good, towards the end of the summer it will really come into its own – by then the vibrant red and purple flowers of the geranium, *Salvia* and lavenders will be at their most prolific.

MATERIALS
60 cm (24 in) wooden planter, stained black
Polystyrene or other suitable drainage material
Compost
Slow-release plant food granules

PLANTS
Geranium (*Pelargonium*) 'Tomcat'
2 *Lavandula pinnata*
2 *Salvia* 'Raspberry Royal'
2 blue *Brachycome* daisies
Convolvulus sabatius
6 rose-pink alyssum

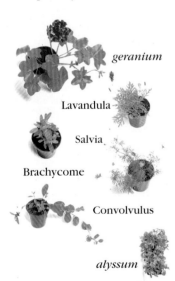

geranium

Lavandula

Salvia

Brachycome

Convolvulus

alyssum

1 Line the base of the container with polystyrene or similar drainage material. Fill the window box with compost, mixing in 3 teaspoons of slow-release plant food granules. Plant the geranium at the back of the window box, in the centre.

2 Plant the two lavenders in the rear corners of the box.

3 Plant the *Salvia* at the front of the box on either side of the geranium.

4 Plant the *Brachycome* daisies in the front corners of the box.

5 Plant the *Convolvulus* in the centre, in front of the geranium.

GARDENER'S TIP

Both the lavenders and the *Salvia* are highly aromatic, so if possible position this box near a door or a path, so that you can enjoy the fragrance as you brush against the plants.

Plant in early summer

6 Fill in the spaces with the alyssum. Water well and place in a sunny position.

A Basket of Pinks

In this basket-weave stone planter sugar-pink petunias are planted with ivy-leaved geraniums and shaggy-flowered pink *Dianthus* with a deep-red eye. None of these plants requires much depth for its roots and provided the plants are fed and watered regularly they will be perfectly happy.

GARDENER'S TIP
Once the summer is over, the petunias and geraniums will need to be removed, but the *Dianthus* will overwinter quite happily. Cut off any flower stems and add a fresh layer of gravel.

Plant in late spring or early summer

MATERIALS
60 cm (24 in) window box
Washed gravel
Compost
Slow-release plant food granules

PLANTS
2 pink-flowered ivy-leaved geraniums (*Pelargoniums*)
3 sugar-pink petunias
6 pink *Dianthus*

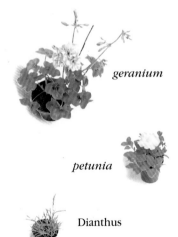

geranium

petunia

Dianthus

1 Fill the base of the window box with a layer of gravel or similar drainage material.

2 Fill the window box with compost, mixing in 2 teaspoons of slow-release plant food granules.

3 Plant the two geraniums about 10 cm (4 in) from either end of the window box.

4 Plant the petunias, evenly spaced, along the back edge of the window box.

5 Plant four of the *Dianthus* along the front edge of the window box and the other two plants on either side of the central petunia.

6 Spread a layer of gravel around the plants; this is decorative and also helps to retain moisture. Water well and stand in a sunny position.

Hot Flowers in a Cool Container

Shocking-pink petunias and verbenas are the dominant plants in this window box which also features softer pink marguerites and silver *Helichrysum*. The dark green of the wooden window box is a calming influence which contrasts pleasingly with the vibrant flowers.

MATERIALS
76 cm (30 in) plastic window box
90 cm (3 ft) wooden window box (optional)
Compost
Slow-release plant food granules

PLANTS
Trailing pink marguerite (*Argyranthemum*) 'Flamingo'
2 bright pink verbenas, such as 'Sissinghurst'
3 shocking-pink petunias
4 *Helichrysum petiolare microphyllum*

marguerite

verbena

petunia

Helichrysum

Plant in late spring or early summer

1 Check the drainage holes are open in the base and, if not, drill or punch them open. Fill the window box with compost, mixing in 3 teaspoons of slow-release plant food granules. Plant the marguerite centre front.

2 Plant the verbenas in the back corners of the window box.

3 Plant one of the petunias behind the marguerite and the other two on either side of it.

4 Plant one *Helichrysum* on each side of the central petunia and the other two *Helichrysum* in the front corners of the window box. Water well and lift into place in the wooden window box, if using. Stand in a sunny position.

Illusions of Grandeur

A small plastic window box takes on unexpected grandeur when filled with rich, velvety purples and pinks and placed in an interesting setting.

MATERIALS
30 cm (12 in) plastic window box
Compost
Slow-release plant food granules

PLANTS
Heliotrope
2 *Viola* 'Bowles' Black'
Blue verbena
4 lilac lobelia

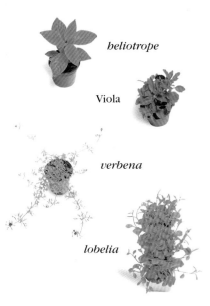

heliotrope

Viola

verbena

lobelia

GARDENER'S TIP
Dead-head the violas regularly to keep them flowering and pinch out any straggly stems.

Plant in spring

1 Check the drainage holes are open in the base and, if not, drill or punch them open. Fill the container with compost, mixing in a teaspoon of slow-release plant food granules. Plant the heliotrope in the centre of the window box at the back.

2 Plant the violas at either end of the window box in the back corners.

3 Plant the verbena centrally in front of the heliotrope.

4 Plant two of the lobelias on either side of the verbena and the other two between the heliotrope and the violas. Water thoroughly and stand in partial shade.

Filigree Foliage

The purply-black leaves of the *Heuchera* are all the more stunning when surrounded by the delicate silver-and-green filigree foliage of *Senecio*, the tender lavender *pinnata* and the soft lilac-coloured flowers of the *Bacopa* and the *Brachycome* daisies. The plants are grown in a white plastic planter which is concealed by an elegant wooden window box.

GARDENER'S TIP

This wooden window box can be set up to be self-watering and is ideal where access is difficult for daily watering. A variety of self-watering containers are available and come with full instructions on how they work.

Plant in spring

MATERIALS
76 cm (30 in) plastic window box
Compost
Slow-release plant food granules
90 cm (3 ft) wooden window box (optional)

PLANTS
Heuchera 'Palace Purple'
2 *Lavandula pinnata*
2 blue *Brachycome* daisies
3 *Senecio Cineraria* 'Silver Dust'
2 blue *Bacopa*

Heuchera

Lavandula

Brachycome

Senecio

Bacopa

1 Check drainage holes are open in base of planter and, if not, drill or punch them out. Fill the window box with compost, mixing in 2 teaspoons of slow-release plant food granules. Plant the *Heuchera* in the centre.

4 Plant the three *Senecio* at the front of the box next to the *Brachycome*.

2 Plant the two lavenders on either side of the *Heuchera*.

5 Plant the two *Bacopa* between the *Senecio* and the *Heuchera*.

3 Plant the two *Brachycome* daisies at either end of the window box.

6 Water thoroughly and lift into place in the wooden window box, if using. Place in full or partial sun.

Wedding Bells

A painted wooden window box filled with a white geranium, verbena, marguerites, *Bacopa* and silver *Senecio* is an ideal combination of plants for a summer wedding celebration in the garden.

GARDENER'S TIP

To prolong the life of wooden containers it is advisable to empty them of compost before winter and store them under cover until spring

Plant in late spring or early summer

MATERIALS
45 cm (18 in) slatted wooden window box
Sphagnum moss
Compost
Slow-release plant food granules

PLANTS
White geranium (*Pelargonium*)
2 white marguerites (*Argyranthemum*)
2 white trailing verbena
2 *Senecio cineraria* 'Silver Dust'
White *Bacopa*

geranium

marguerite

verbena

Senecio

Bacopa

1 It is a good idea to line slatted wooden containers with moss before planting to prevent the compost from leaking out.

2 Fill the moss-lined window box with compost, mixing in 2 teaspoons of slow-release plant food granules. Plant the geranium in the centre of the window box towards the back.

3 Plant the marguerites on either side of the geranium.

4 Plant the verbenas in the two back corners of the window box.

5 Plant the *Senecio* in the front two corners of the window box.

6 Plant the *Bacopa* centrally in the front of the box. Water thoroughly and stand in a sunny position.

EDIBLE BOXES

Herbs for a Sunny Position

Choose herbs that enjoy the same conditions and you will have a window box that looks good throughout the summer. Here, sun-loving herbs such as rosemary, sage, marjoram and two varieties of thyme are planted together.

GARDENER'S TIP
Herbs are at their most flavoursome and aromatic before they flower, so as soon as the plants are well-established you can start picking them for use in the kitchen.

Plant in early spring

MATERIALS
36 cm (14 in) wooden window box
Clay granules or other suitable drainage material
Compost
Slow-release plant food granules, pelleted chicken manure, or similar organic plant food

PLANTS
Marjoram
Prostrate rosemary, such as 'Tuscan Blue'
Lemon thyme (*Thymus* x *citriodorus*) 'Archer's Gold'
Common thyme (*Thymus vulgaris*)
Sage (*Salvia officinalis*) 'Tricolor'

marjoram

rosemary

lemon thyme

common thyme

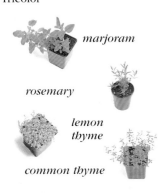
sage

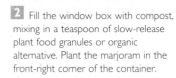

1 Fill the base of the window box with clay granules or similar suitable drainage material.

2 Fill the window box with compost, mixing in a teaspoon of slow-release plant food granules or organic alternative. Plant the marjoram in the front-right corner of the container.

3 Plant the rosemary centre front.

4 Plant the lemon thyme in the front-left corner of the window box.

5 Plant the common thyme at the back of the window box between the rosemary and the marjoram.

6 Plant the sage between the lemon thyme and the rosemary at the back of the window box. Water well and stand in full sun.

Herbs in the Shade

Although the Mediterranean herbs need lots of sunshine, there are many others which prefer a cooler situation to look and taste their best. This window box, ideal for just outside the kitchen door or window, has an interesting variety of mints, sorrel, chives, lemon balm and parsley.

GARDENER'S TIP
Use the freshly picked mint to make refreshing teas. Pour recently boiled water over a few washed leaves and infuse for five minutes.

Plant in early spring

MATERIALS
50 cm (20 in) terracotta window box
Polystyrene or other suitable drainage material
Compost
Slow-release plant food granules, pelleted chicken manure, or similar organic plant food

PLANTS
Lemon balm (*Melissa officinalis*)
3 mints (black peppermint, silver mint and curly spearmint were used here)
Sorrel
Chives
Parsley

lemon balm

mint

sorrel

chives

parsley

1 Fill the base of the container with polystyrene or similar suitable drainage material. Fill the window box with compost, mixing in 3 teaspoons of slow-release plant food granules or organic alternative.

2 Plant the lemon balm in the back right-hand corner.

3 Plant two of the mints along the back of the window box and the third in the front right-hand corner of the container.

4 Plant the sorrel in the middle of the window box at the front.

5 Plant the chives at the front in the left-hand corner.

6 Finally, plant the parsley between the sorrel and the mint. Position in light shade. Water thoroughly.

Vital Ingredients

A lovely present for an enthusiastic cook, this window box contains chervil, coriander, fennel, garlic, purple sage, French tarragon, savory, origanum and basil.

MATERIALS
45 cm (18 in) wooden window box
Crocks or other suitable drainage material
Compost
Slow-release plant food granules, pelleted chicken manure, or similar organic plant food

PLANTS
French tarragon
Chervil
Garlic
Coriander
Purple sage
Basil
Fennel
Savory (*Satureja hortensis*)
Origanum

French tarragon

chervil

garlic

coriander

purple sage

basil

fennel

savory

origanum

1 Line the base of the container with crocks or other suitable drainage material. Fill the window box with compost, mixing in a teaspoon of slow-release plant food granules or organic alternative.

2 Before planting the herbs, arrange them in the window box in their pots.

Plant in spring

3 Plant the back row of herbs first.

4 Plant more herbs at the front of the window box. Water well and stand in a sunny position.

A Strawberry Bed in Miniature

Strawberries are a pretty and tempting alternative to flowers in a window box. The strawberries will benefit from being planted in the garden at the end of the summer; in the meantime, they make good ornamental plants in a window box or even a moss-lined wicker basket. The addition of alpine strawberries gives a pleasant variation of scale.

MATERIALS
36 cm (14 in) basket
Moss
Compost
Slow-release plant food granules, pelleted chicken manure or other organic plant food

PLANTS
2 strawberry plants 'Maxim', or similar
2 alpine strawberry plants

strawberry

alpine strawberry

GARDENER'S TIP
To ensure a good crop next year, the leaves of the large strawberries should be cut right back after fruiting.

Plant in early spring

1 Line the basket with a generous layer of moss – this will prevent the compost leaking away.

2 Fill the basket with compost, mixing in a teaspoon of slow-release plant food granules or the organic alternative.

3 Plant the large strawberry plants at either end of the basket.

4 Plant the alpine strawberries in the middle. Water thoroughly and stand in a sunny position.

The Good Life

This window box will not exactly make you self-sufficient, but it is surprising how many different vegetables can be grown in a small space. It is perfect for anyone who likes the taste of home-grown vegetables but does not have a garden to grow them in.

GARDENER'S TIP
It is now possible to buy "plugs" of small vegetable plants at garden centres. There is no need to separate the plants provided there is sufficient room between the clumps.

Plant in spring

MATERIALS
76 cm (30 in) plastic window box
Compost
Slow-release plant food granules, pelleted chicken manure or similar organic plant food

PLANTS
Garlic
3 Chinese leaves
4 plugs of beetroot (see Gardener's Tip)
Pepper plant
3 dwarf French beans
3 plugs of shallots

garlic

Chinese leaves

beetroot

pepper

dwarf French beans

shallots

1 Check the drainage holes are open in the base and, if not, drill or punch them open. Fill the window box with compost, mixing in 2 teaspoons of slow-release plant food granules or an organic alternative. Starting at the right-hand end of the window box, first plant the garlic.

4 Plant the pepper plant next, just to the left of the centre.

2 Next plant the Chinese leaves.

5 Now plant the three dwarf French bean plants.

3 Follow this with the plugs of beetroot.

6 Finally, plant the shallot plugs in the left-hand corner. Water well and stand in full or partial sun.

A Taste for Flowers

It is often said that something "looks good enough to eat" and in this instance it is true. All the flowers in this window box may be used for flavour and garnishes provided, of course, that they are washed.

MATERIALS
36 cm (14 in) terracotta window box
Crocks or other suitable drainage material
Compost
Slow-release plant food granules, pelleted chicken manure or similar organic plant food

PLANTS
Chives
2 nasturtiums
2 pansies with well-marked "faces"
2 pot marigolds (*Calendula*)

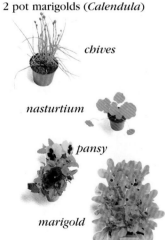

chives

nasturtium

pansy

marigold

GARDENER'S TIP
To keep all the plants producing flowers, dead-head regularly. Once a plant has set seed it considers its work done and will produce fewer and fewer flowers.

Plant in early spring

1 Cover the base of the window box with a layer of crocks or similar drainage material. Fill with compost, mixing in 2 teaspoons of slow-release plant food granules or organic alternative. Plant the chives in the right-hand corner.

2 Plant one of the nasturtiums in the left-hand corner and the other centre front.

3 Plant one pansy at the back next to the chives and the other at the front to the left of the central nasturtium.

4 Plant one of the marigolds at the back between the pansy and nasturtium and the other one just behind the central nasturtium.

Home-grown Salads

These compact but heavy-fruiting tomato plants have been specially bred to be grown in containers. Teamed with lettuce, radishes, chives and parsley, they provide all the ingredients for a fresh garden salad.

MATERIALS
76 cm (30 in) plastic window
  box
Compost
Slow-release plant food granules,
  pelleted chicken manure or
  similar organic plant food

PLANTS
3 tomatoes 'Tumbler', or similar
  compact variety
Chives
4 lettuces, 'Little Gem' and
  'Corsair' are recommended
2 Salad Bowl lettuces
4 parsley plants
Radish seed

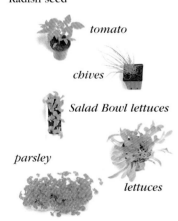

tomato

chives

Salad Bowl lettuces

parsley

lettuces

GARDENER'S TIP
Keep the tomato plants watered at all times and liquid feed with a proprietary tomato food or liquid seaweed fertilizer.

Plant in spring

1 Check the drainage holes are open in the base and, if not, drill or punch them open. Fill the window box with compost, mixing in 2 teaspoons of slow-release plant food granules or organic alternative. Plant the tomatoes, evenly spaced, along the central line of the window box.

2 Plant the chives in front of the middle tomato plant. Plant the Little Gem or Corsair lettuces diagonally from one another between the tomato plants.

3 Plant the Salad Bowl lettuces in the front corners of the window box. Plant the parsley plants diagonally opposite one another alongside the Little Gem or Corsair lettuces.

4 Scatter radish seed between the plants and gently rake into the soil. Water thoroughly and stand in a sunny position.

SCENTED BOXES

A Nose-twitcher Window Box

One of the French country names for the nasturtium means 'nose-twitcher' and refers to the peppery smell of the plant. It has been planted here with the equally aromatic and colourful ginger mint and pot marigold.

MATERIALS
25 cm (10 in) terracotta window
  box
Crocks or other suitable
  drainage material
Compost
Slow-release plant food granules

PLANTS
Variegated ginger mint
Nasturtium 'Empress of India',
  or similar
Pot marigold (*Calendula*)
  'Gitana', or similar compact
  form

ginger mint

nasturtium

marigold

GARDENER'S TIP
A small window box like this one can double as a table centre-piece for an outdoor meal.

Plant in spring

1 Cover the base of the window box with a layer of crocks or similar drainage material. Fill the container with compost, mixing in a half-teaspoon of slow-release plant food granules.

2 Plant the ginger mint on the right of the container.

3 Plant the nasturtium in the centre.

4 Plant the marigold on the left of the container. Water well and stand in full or partial sun.

Sweet-smelling Summer Flowers

Scented geranium and verbena are combined with heliotrope and petunias to make a window box that is a fragrant as well as a visual pleasure.

MATERIALS
40 cm (16 in) terracotta window
  box
Crocks or other suitable
  drainage material
Compost
Slow-release plant food granules

PLANTS
Scented-leaf geranium
  (*Pelargonium*) 'Lady Plymouth'
3 soft pink petunias
Heliotrope
2 *Verbena* 'Pink Parfait'

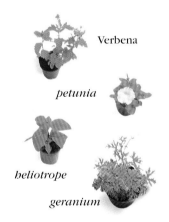

Verbena

petunia

heliotrope

geranium

GARDENER'S TIP
At the end of the summer the geranium can be potted up and kept through the winter as a houseplant. Reduce the height of the plant by at least a half and it will soon send out new shoots.

Plant in late spring or early summer

1 Cover the base of the window box with a layer of crocks. Fill with compost, mixing in 2 teaspoons of slow-release plant food granules. Plant the geranium to the right of centre, towards the back of the window box.

2 Plant a petunia in each corner and one in the centre at the front of the window box.

3 Plant the heliotrope to the left of the geranium.

4 Plant one verbena behind the heliotrope and the other in front of the geranium. Water well and place in a sunny position.

Scented Geraniums

There is a wonderful variation in leaf size, shape and colouring as well as an incredible diversity of scents amongst the *Pelargonium* family. Choose the fragrances you like best and put the plants where you will brush against them to release their fragrance.

MATERIALS
40 cm (16 in) terracotta window box
Crocks or other suitable drainage material
Compost
Slow-release plant food granules

PLANTS
4 scented-leaf geraniums (*Pelargonium fragrans*)

geraniums

1 Cover the base of the window box with a layer of crocks or other suitable drainage material. Fill with compost, mixing in 2 teaspoons of slow-release plant food granules. Plant the first geranium at the right-hand end of the container.

2 Choose a contrasting leaf colour and shape and plant this next to the first geranium towards the front edge of the window box.

3 Plant the third geranium behind the second geranium.

GARDENER'S TIP
During the summer, pick and dry the leaves of these geraniums for use in pot-pourri or in muslin bags to scent linen. If you have a greenhouse or conservatory, move the window box inside for the winter and water sparingly until spring.

Plant in spring

4 Finally, plant the fourth geranium at the left-hand end of the container. Water well and position in full or partial sun.

A Butterfly Garden

We should all do our bit to encourage butterflies into our gardens and this window box with sedum, marjoram, thyme and origanum should prove irresistible. All these plants are perennials and can be over-wintered in the window box.

GARDENER'S TIP
You can imitate the look of an old stone window box by painting a new one with a dilute mixture of liquid seaweed plant food and water. This encourages moss to grow and "ages" the stone.

Plant in spring

MATERIALS
60 cm (24 in) stone window
  box
Crocks or other suitable
  drainage material
Compost
Slow-release plant food granules

PLANTS
Sedum 'Ruby Glow'
Marjoram
Lemon thyme (*Thymus
  citriodorus*)
Common thyme (*Thymus
  vulgaris*)
Origanum

Sedum

marjoram

*lemon
thyme*

common thyme

origanum

1 Cover the base of the window box with a layer of crocks or other suitable drainage material. Fill with compost, mixing in 3 teaspoons of slow-release plant food granules.

2 Plant the sedum off-centre to the left of the window box.

3 Plant the marjoram to the left of the sedum.

4 Plant the lemon thyme in the centre at the front of the window box.

5 Plant the common thyme in the back right-hand corner of the container.

6 Plant the origanum in the front right-hand corner of the window box. Water well and place in a sunny position.

The Apothecary Box

Many plants have healing qualities and, while they should always be used with caution, some of the more commonly used herbs have been successful country remedies for centuries.

GARDENER'S TIP
Herbs should not be used to treat an existing medical condition without first checking with your medical practitioner.

Plant in the spring

MATERIALS
Wooden trug
Compost
2 tsp pelleted chicken manure or similar organic plant food

PLANTS
Lavender – for relaxing
Rosemary – for healthy hair and scalp
Chamomile – for restful sleep
Fennel – for digestion
Feverfew (*Matricaria*) – for migraine
3 pot marigolds (*Calendula*) – for healing

lavender

rosemary

chamomile

fennel

feverfew

pot marigold

1 Place a layer of drainage material in the trug and fill with compost, mixing in 2 teaspoons of fertilizer.

2 Plant the lavender in the centre of the trug and the rosemary in the front right-hand corner.

3 Plant the chamomile in the back left-hand corner.

4 Plant the fennel in the back right-hand corner.

5 Plant the feverfew in the front left-hand corner.

6 Plant the marigolds in the spaces between the other herbs. Water well and stand in full or partial sun.

SEASONAL BOXES

Spring Flowers in an Instant

An arrangement of pots of spring flowers is surrounded with bark to give the appearance of a planted window box. As soon as the flowers are over, the pots can be removed and the container is ready for its summer planting.

MATERIALS
40 cm (16 in) terracotta window
  box
Bark

PLANTS
Pot of daffodils
Pot of yellow tulips
4 yellow pansies in pots

daffodil

tulip

pansy

GARDENER'S TIP
Once the flowers have finished and the pots have been removed from the window box, the pots of bulbs can be tucked in a corner of the garden ready to flower again next year.

Plant in late winter or early spring

1 Position the pot of daffodils at the right-hand end of the window box.

2 Position the tulips at the left-hand end of the window box.

3 Fill around the pots with bark until the window box is half-full.

4 Position the pansies between the tulips and the daffodils and add bark until all the pots are concealed. Water moderately and stand in any position.

A Spring Display of Auriculas

An old strawberry punnet carrier makes an attractive and unusual window box in which to display some beautifully marked auriculas planted in antique terracotta pots. A large flower basket or wooden trug would look just as good as this old wooden carrier.

MATERIALS
50 cm (20 in) wooden carrier
10 8-10 cm (3-4 in) old or
  antique-style terracotta pots
Crocks
Compost

PLANTS
10 different auriculas (*Primula auricula*)

auriculas

GARDENER'S TIP
A windowsill is an ideal position to see auriculas at their best. It is difficult to admire the full drama of their markings if they are at ground level. When they have finished flowering, stand the pots in a shady corner or a cold frame.

Plant in early spring

1 Place a crock over the drainage hole of a pot.

2 Remove a plant from its plastic pot and plant it firmly with added compost.

3 Stand the newly planted auricula in the wooden carrier.

4 Repeat the process for the other flowers. Water thoroughly and stand in light shade.

Sea View

While all these plants are most at home in a seaside environment, they are also happy on a hot windowsill away from the coast. Scatter a few seashells around them and you have got your own private beach!

MATERIALS
45 cm (18 in) terracotta tray
4 10 cm (4 in) terracotta pots
Crocks
Compost
Slow-release plant food granules
Gravel
Seashells

PLANTS
Orange *Gazania*
2 yellow *Osteospermum*
Yellow *Portulaca*

Gazania

Osteospermum

Portulaca

GARDENER'S TIP
At the end of the summer the *Gazania* and *Osteospermums* can be overwintered by cutting them back and keeping them fairly dry in a frost-free environment. Next spring they can be planted out in the garden.

Plant in late spring or early summer

1 Plant the *Gazania* in a terracotta pot. When potting in terracotta, place a crock over the drainage hole in the base of the pot.

2 Plant each *Osteospermum* in a terracotta pot.

3 Plant the *Portulaca* in a terracotta pot. When all the plants are re-potted, divide a teaspoon of plant food granules between the four pots, working them into the top layer of compost.

4 Cover the tray with a layer of gravel.

5 Arrange the plants on the tray.

6 Mulch the pots with gravel and add seashells to the pots and the tray. Water well and stand in a sunny position.

Evergreens and Extra Colour

They may be easy to look after but all-year-round window boxes can start to look a bit life-less after a couple of seasons. It does not take much trouble to add a few seasonal flowers and it can make all the difference.

GARDENER'S TIP
At the end of the summer, remove the *Diascias* and marguerite, feed the remaining plants with more granules and fill the spaces with winter-flowering plants such as pansies or heathers.

Plant in spring

MATERIALS
76 cm (30 in) plastic window box
Compost
Slow-release plant food granules

PLANTS
Hebe 'Baby Marie'
Convolvulus cneorum
Potentilla 'Nunk'
Variegated ivies
2 *Diascia* 'Ruby Field'
Pink marguerite (*Argyranthemum*) 'Flamingo'

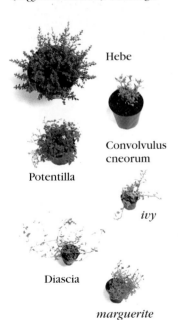

Hebe

Convolvulus cneorum

Potentilla

ivy

Diascia

marguerite

1 Check the drainage holes are open in the base and, if not, drill or punch them open. Fill the window box with compost, mixing in 3 teaspoons of slow-release plant food granules. Plant the *Hebe* in the centre.

2 Plant the *Convolvulus* near the right-hand end of the window box.

3 Plant the *Potentilla* near the left-hand end of the window box.

4 Plant the two ivies at the front corners of the window box.

5 Plant the *Diascias* on either side of the *Hebe* at the front of the window box.

6 Plant the marguerite between the *Hebe* and the *Convolvulus* at the back of the window box. Water well and stand in full or partial sun.

Winter Cheer

Many window boxes are left unplanted through the winter, but you can soon brighten the house or garden for the winter season with this easy arrangement of pot-grown plants plunged in bark.

MATERIALS
40 cm (16 in) glazed window box
Bark

PLANTS
2 miniature conifers
2 variegated ivies
2 red polyanthus

miniature conifer

ivy

polyanthus

1 Water all the plants. Place the conifers, still in their pots, at either end of the window box.

2 Half-fill the window box with bark.

3 Place the pots of polyanthus on the bark between the two conifers.

4 Place the pots of ivy on the bark in the front corners of the window box. Add further bark to the container until all the pots are concealed. Water only when plants show signs of dryness. Stand in any position.

GARDENER'S TIP
When it is time to replant the window box, plunge the conifers, still in their pots, in a shady position in the garden. Water well through the spring and summer and they may be used again next year.

Plant in early winter

BOXES FOR DIFFICULT SPOTS

Shady Characters

All the plants used in this window box are perfectly happy in the shade. A periwinkle with variegated leaves and blue spring flowers is planted with blue-leaved hostas and summer-flowering busy lizzies in a window box that will brighten a gloomy corner for many months.

MATERIALS
45 cm (18 in) fibre window box
Crocks or other suitable drainage
  material
Compost
Slow-release plant food granules

PLANTS
Variegated periwinkle (*Vinca minor* 'Aureovariegata')
3 *Hosta* 'Blue Moon'
5 white busy lizzies (*Impatiens*)

periwinkle

Hosta

busy lizzie

GARDENER'S TIP
To keep the busy lizzies looking their best, pick off the dead flowers and leaves regularly or they will stick to the plant and spoil its appearance.

Plant in late spring

1 Cover the base of the window box with a layer of drainage material. Fill the window box with compost, mixing in 2 teaspoons of slow-release plant food granules.

2 Plant the periwinkle in the centre of the box.

3 Plant two of the hostas in the back corners of the window box and the third in front of, or slightly to one side of, the periwinkle.

4 Plant the busy lizzies in the spaces between the other plants.

Shade-loving Ferns

This window box is ideal for a dark, damp and shady spot – conditions that many plants dislike but much loved by ferns. Provided the plants are not allowed to dry out too often they will grow happily for many years.

MATERIALS
40 cm (16 in) glazed window
  box
Clay granules or other suitable
  drainage material
Compost
Slow-release plant food granules
Bark

PLANTS
A selection of three ferns

ferns

1 Cover the base of the container with a layer of drainage material.

2 Plant the first fern in the left-hand end of the container

GARDENER'S TIP

In the autumn when the leaves begin to die back, cut back all the foliage and apply a fresh layer of bark to protect the plants over winter. Feed in the spring.

Plant in spring

3 Plant the second fern centrally.

4 Plant the third fern at the right-hand end of the window box. Mulch with bark and water thoroughly. Stand in a cool position.

A Dazzling Display

The succulents in this window box will provide a vivid splash of colour throughout the summer and are ideal for a hot dry windowsill. *Mesembryanthemums*, *Kalanchoë* and *Portulaca* all love the sunshine and will grow happily in this small window box.

MATERIALS
36 cm (14 in) plastic window box
Compost
Slow-release plant food granules

PLANTS
Kalanchoë
2 *Portulaca*
3 *Mesembryanthemum*

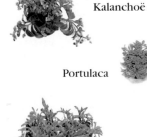

Kalanchoë

Portulaca

Mesembryanthemum

1 Check the drainage holes are open in the base and, if not, drill or punch them open. Fill the window box with compost, mixing in a teaspoon of slow-release plant food granules.

2 Plant the *Kalanchoë* in the centre of the window box.

3 Plant the two *Portulaca* in the front corners of the window box.

GARDENER'S TIP

Mesembryanthemums open daily in response to direct sunlight so it is essential to place them in a position where they are in full sun for as long as possible.

Plant in late spring or early summer

4 Plant one *Mesembryanthemum* in front of the *Kalanchoë* and the other two behind the two *Portulaca*. Water well and stand in a sunny position.

Desert Belles

An attractively weathered window box is the container used for this dramatic collection of succulents. With their architectural leaf shapes and wonderful range of colouring they would look particularly good in a contemporary setting.

GARDENER'S TIP

Move the window box to a conservatory or frost-free greenhouse for the winter. Water sparingly only if plants show signs of shrivelling.

Plant in late spring or early summer for outdoor use, any time of year for a conservatory

MATERIALS
40 cm (16 in) terracotta window
  box
Crocks or other suitable
  drainage material
Compost
Gravel
Slow-release plant food granules

PLANTS
Aloe
Crassula ovata
Echeveria elegans
Sansevieria trifasciata

Aloe

Crassula ovata

Echeveria elegans

*Sansevieria
trifasciata*

1 Place a layer of crocks or other suitable drainage material in the base of the container.

2 Fill with compost, mixing in a teaspoon of slow-release plant food granules. Plant the aloe at the right-hand end of the window box.

3 Plant the *Crassula* next to the aloe.

4 Plant the *Echeveria* towards the back of the container, next to the *Crassula*.

5 Plant the *Sansevieria* in front of the *Echeveria*.

6 Surround the plants with a layer of gravel. Water well to establish and thereafter water sparingly. Place in full sun.

INSPIRATIONAL BOXES

Old Favourites

Dianthus, violas and candytuft are delightful cottage-garden plants and make a pretty display during late spring and early summer. Although by the time we took our photograph the candytuft had finished flowering the other flowers were still putting on a good show.

MATERIALS
40 cm (16 in) painted wooden
  window box
Crocks or other suitable
  drainage material
Compost
Slow-release plant food granules

PLANTS
Dianthus
Candytuft (*Iberis*)
2 violas

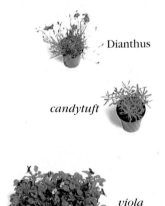
Dianthus

candytuft

viola

1 Cover the base of the container with a layer of drainage material. Fill with compost, mixing in a teaspoon of slow-release plant food granules.

2 Plant the *Dianthus* slightly to the right of the centre of the window box.

3 Plant the candytuft to the left of the centre of the window box.

4 Plant a viola at each end. Water well and stand in a mixture of sun and shade.

GARDENER'S TIP
Once the flowers are over, cut the plants back and plant them out in the garden. There is still time to replant the window box with summer plants.

Plant in early spring

Colourful Evergreens

Evergreen *Cordyline*, with its dramatic red spear-shaped leaves, a green *Hebe* and a golden conifer have been mixed with blue-green hostas in a permanent planting, which is given seasonal interest by the addition of red-flowered New Guinea *Impatiens*.

GARDENER'S TIP
At the end of the summer replace the *Impatiens* with pansies, polyanthus or heathers.

Plant in spring

MATERIALS
76 cm (30 in) plastic window
 box
Compost
Slow-release plant food granules

PLANTS
Red *Cordyline*
Golden conifer *Chamaecyparis
 pisifera* 'Sungold'
Hebe 'Emerald Gem'
Hosta 'Blue Moon'
Golden grass *Hakonechloa*
 'Aureola'
2 red-flowered New Guinea
 Impatiens

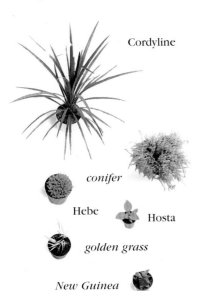

Cordyline

conifer

Hebe

Hosta

golden grass

New Guinea
Impatiens

1 Check the drainage holes are open in the base and, if not, drill or punch them open. Fill the window box with compost, mixing in 3 teaspoons of slow-release plant food granules. Plant the *Cordyline* half-way from the centre of the window box on the left-hand side.

4 Plant the hosta between the *Hebe* and the conifer.

2 Plant the conifer at the right-hand end of the window box.

5 Plant the golden grass at the left-hand end of the window box.

3 Plant the *Hebe* in the centre of the window box.

6 Plant the *Impatiens* between the golden grass and the *Cordyline* and next to the hosta. Water well and stand in partial sun.

A Topiary Planting

Topiary box plants remain in their pots in this window box. A mulch of bark conceals the pots and retains moisture, and small pots of white *Bacopa* add another dimension to this simple design.

MATERIALS
64 cm (25 in) terracotta planter
Bark

PLANTS
Box pyramid in 5-litre (9 in) pot
2 box balls in 5-litre (9 in) pots
5 pots white *Bacopa*

box pyramid

box balls

Bacopa

1 Water all the plants thoroughly. Stand the box pyramid in the centre of the container.

2 Stand the box balls on either side of the pyramid.

3 Fill the container with bark.

4 Plunge the pots of *Bacopa* in the bark at the front of the container. Stand in light shade. Water regularly.

GARDENER'S TIP

Provided the box plants are not root-bound they will be quite happy in their pots for a year. If the leaves start to lose their glossy dark green colour, it is a sign that the plants need a feed. Sprinkle a long-term plant feed on the surface of the pots and boost with a liquid feed.

Plant box at any time of year, and Bacopa *in spring*

Topiary Ivy with White Petunias

Use wire topiary frames (available at most garden centres) to train ivy or other climbing plants into interesting shapes. The ivy will take some months to really establish its outline; in the meantime, miniature white petunias complete the picture.

GARDENER'S TIP
Maintain the shape of the ivy with regular trimming and training – five minutes once a week will create a better shape than 15 minutes once a month.

Plant ivy at any time of year, petunias in spring

MATERIALS
45 cm (18 in) oval terracotta window box
Crocks or other suitable drainage material
Compost
Slow-release plant food granules
Wire topiary frame
Pins made from garden wire
Plant rings

PLANTS
2 variegated ivies
4 miniature white petunias

ivies

petunia

1 Place a layer of drainage material in the base of the window box. Fill the window box with compost, mixing in 2 teaspoons of slow-release plant food granules.

2 Plant the two ivies, one in front of the other in the centre of the window box.

3 Position the topiary frame in the centre of the window box and use pins to hold it in place.

4 Wrap the stems of ivy around the stem of the frame and then around the frame itself.

5 Cut away any straggly stems and use plant rings to secure the ivy to the frame.

6 Plant the petunias around the topiary ivy. Water thoroughly and stand in light shade.

A Trough of Alpines

A selection of easy-to-grow alpine plants are grouped in a basket-weave stone planter to create a miniature garden. The mulch of gravel is both attractive and practical as it prevents soil splashing on to the leaves of the plants.

MATERIALS
40 cm (16 in) stone trough
Crocks or other suitable
 drainage material
Compost
Slow-release plant food granules
Gravel

PLANTS
Sempervivum
Alpine *Aquilegia*
White rock rose (*Helianthemum*)
Papaver alpinum
Alpine phlox
Pink saxifrage
White saxifrage

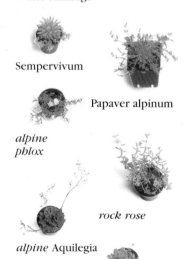

Sempervivum

Papaver alpinum

alpine phlox

rock rose

alpine Aquilegia

saxifrage

1 Cover the base of the trough with a layer of crocks.

2 Fill the container with compost, mixing in a teaspoon of slow-release plant food granules and extra gravel for improved drainage.

3 Before planting, arrange the plants, still in their pots, in the trough to decide on the most attractive arrangement.

4 Start planting from one end, working across the trough.

5 Complete the planting.

6 Scatter a good layer of gravel around the plants. Water thoroughly and stand in a sunny position.

White Flowers and Painted Terracotta

There are plenty of inexpensive window boxes available, but they do tend to be rather similar. Why not customize a bought window box to give it a touch of individuality? This deep-blue painted window box creates an interesting setting for the cool white geraniums and verbenas.

MATERIALS
45 cm (18 in) terracotta window box painted blue
Crocks or other suitable drainage material
Compost
Slow release plant food granules

PLANTS
White geranium (*Pelargonium*)
2 variegated *Felicia*
2 white trailing verbena

geranium

Felicia

verbena

1 Cover the base of the window box with a layer of crocks or similar drainage material.

2 Fill the window box with compost, mixing in 2 teaspoons of slow-release plant food granules. Plant the geranium in the centre of the window box.

3 Plant a *Felicia* on either side of the geranium at the back of the container.

4 Plant a verbena on either side of the geranium at the front of the window box. Water well and stand in a sunny position.

GARDENER'S TIP
White geraniums need regular dead-heading to look their best. Old flowerheads discolour and spoil the appearance of the plant.

Plant in late spring or early summer

Daring Reds and Bold Purples

The colour of the fuchsia flowers is echoed by the deep purple and crimson petunias in this window box, which also includes trailing campanula and catmint.

GARDENER'S TIP

At the end of the season the catmint plants can be trimmed back and planted in the garden. The fuchsia and *Campanulas* can be cut back and potted up to be overwintered in a frost-free greenhouse.

Plant in spring

MATERIALS

76 cm (30 in) plastic window box
90 cm (3 ft) wooden window box (optional)
Compost
Slow-release plant food granules

PLANTS

Fuchsia 'Dollar Princess'
2 low-growing catmint (*Nepeta mussinii*)
2 white-flowered *Campanula isophylla*
2 crimson petunias
2 purple petunias

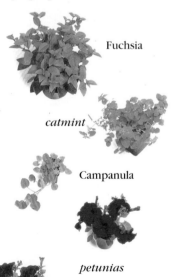

Fuchsia

catmint

Campanula

petunias

1 Check the drainage holes are open in the base and, if not, drill or punch them open. Fill the window box with compost, mixing in 3 teaspoons of slow-release plant food granules. Plant the fuchsia in the centre of the window box.

2 Plant the catmint at either end of the window box.

3 Plant the *Campanula* next to the catmint.

4 Plant the crimson petunias on either side of the fuchsia at the back of the window box.

5 Plant the purple petunias on either side of the fuchsia at the front of the window box. Water thoroughly and allow to drain.

6 Lower the plastic window box into place inside the wooden window box, if using. Stand in a sunny position.

Seasonal Planting Lists

Plants to last into late autumn

Begonias
Felicia
Fuchsias
Geraniums (*Pelargonium*)
Helichrysum
Salvia
Scaevola

Plants for an early spring window box

Crocuses
Ferns
Forget-me-nots (*Myosotis*)
Hyacinths
Ivies
Narcissi and daffodils
Pansies
Periwinkle (*Vinca minor*)
Polyanthus
Primroses
Tulips
Violas

Plants for the summer

Alyssum
Brachycome daisies
Busy lizzies
Campanula
Convolvulus
Dianthus
Felicia
Fuchsias
Heliotropes
Lavenders
Lobelia
Marguerites
Nasturtiums
Osteospermum
Petunias
Pot marigolds (*Calendula*)
Salvia
Tobacco, flowering (*Nicotiana*)
Verbenas
Violas

Plants for winter window boxes

Convolvulus
Ivies
Miniature conifers
Ornamental cabbages
Pansies
Periwinkle (*Vinca minor*)
Polyanthus
Violas

INDEX

Acknowledgments

The author would like to thank By-Pass Nurseries of Mark Tey for supplying many of the plants and taking care of the window boxes until they were ready for photographing. Special thanks to Priscilla, Mervyn, Margaret and Darren.

Thanks also to Les Amis du Jardin, 187 Sussex Gardens, London W2 2RH for the loan of the wooden window boxes.

Thanks to Tree Heritage, North Road, Hertford for the loan of the topiary box.

Sources

Terracotta window boxes supplied by:

The Red Mud Hut, Cockridden Farm Estate, Herringate, Brentwood, Essex

Provenance Plants, 1 Guessens Walk, Welwyn Garden City, Herts AL8 6QS
(Mail order only)

Props supplied by:

Tapestry Antiques, 33 Suffolk Parade, Cheltenham, Glos

SIA – The Shop, 7 Montpelier Avenue, Cheltenham, Glos